Felt and Magnet Crafts

by Judy Walsch

illustrated by Roy Green

STANDARD
PUBLISHING
Cincinnati, Ohio

DEDICATION

This book is dedicated to all the Awana Cubbie Clubs all over the world, and to my wonderful husband, Calvin C. Walsch, and my three lovely children, Calvin, Suzann, and Kathrin.

The Standard Publishing Company, Cincinnati, Ohio
A division of Standex International Corporation

©1992 by The Standard Publishing Company
All rights reserved
Printed in U.S.A.

99 98 97 96 95 94 93 92   5 4 3 2 1

Library of Congress Cataloging-in-Publication Data
    Walsch, Judy.
      Felt and magnet crafts / by Judy Walsch.
        p. cm.
      Includes index.
      ISBN 0-87403-738-7
        1. Felt work. 2. Bible crafts. I. Title.
    TT880.W35 1992
    746'.0463--dc20   92-3719
                  CIP

Contents

TIPS FOR MAKING
FELT AND MAGNET CRAFTS

These pages may be copied for classroom or Bible school use. Each craft includes patterns, Scripture verse, step-by-step instructions, a label, and an illustration of the finished product. Young children will need supervision in making their felt and magnet crafts. An adult should show them correct placement of pre-cut felt parts. Older children might be able to cut their own patterns. When photocopying the patterns, you may want to enlarge them if possible.

ART METHODS
AND MATERIALS USED

Materials used for most of these crafts include felt, paper, thin cardboard or manila folder backing, strips of magnet, glue stick or tacky glue, and scissors. Additional materials may be listed for some crafts. A simple glue stick can be used to attach the felt to the backing, although tacky glue is better for gluing on the eyes. Children could use a small paint brush or popsicle stick to spread glue instead of their fingers. The glue can be stored in a small baby food jar. If you are limited in the amount and variety of felt, feel free to change the suggestions for the felt colors.

Creation Day 1

Scripture: Genesis 1:1-5

Materials: black and white felt; thin cardboard; glue; scissors; magnet strip

Instructions:
1. Photocopy patterns. Cut photocopied patterns out. Trace **1** on thin cardboard and cut out.
2. Trace **2** on black felt. Trace **3** on white felt. Cut out.
3. Cut out **4** and color.
4. Glue **2** on cardboard backing. Glue remaining pieces onto craft using finished illustration as guide.
5. Attach a strip of magnet to the back of the craft.

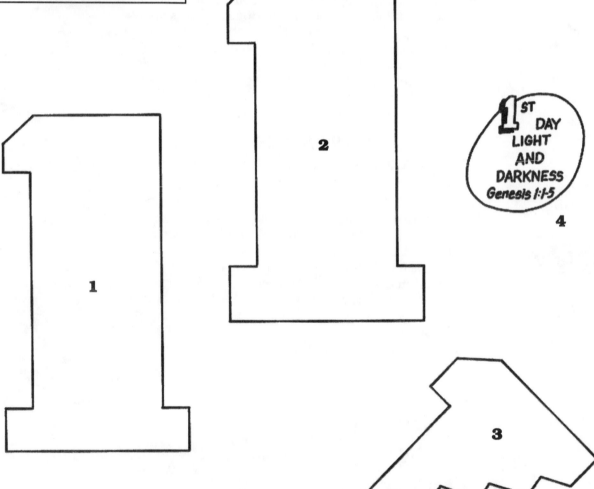

Scripture: Genesis 1:6-8

Materials: dark blue, light blue, and white felt; thin cardboard; glue; scissors; magnet strip

Instructions:
1. Photocopy patterns. Cut photocopied patterns out. Trace **1** on thin cardboard and cut out.
2. Trace **2** on dark blue felt. Trace **3** on light blue felt. Trace **4-7** on white felt. Cut out.
3. Cut out **8** and color.
4. Glue **2** on cardboard backing. Glue remaining pieces onto craft using finished illustration as guide.
5. Attach a strip of magnet to the back of the craft.

Creation Day 3

Scripture: Genesis 1:9-13

Materials: light blue, green, light green, and various colored felt pieces; thin cardboard; glue; scissors; small twig; magnet strip

Instructions:

1. Photocopy patterns. Cut photocopied patterns out. Trace **1** on thin cardboard. Cut out.
2. Trace **2** on light blue felt. Trace **3** and **4** on green felt. Trace **5** on light green felt. Trace **6** and **7** a few times each on various colored felt. Cut out.
3. Cut out **8** and color.
4. Glue **2** on cardboard backing. Glue **3** over bottom half of **2**. Glue twig in position indicated on finished illustration. Glue **4** over twig. Glue **5** over **4**. Glue **6** and **7** over various places on **3**. Glue **8** in position indicated in finished illustration.
5. Attach a strip of magnet to the back of the craft.

Creation Day 6

Scripture: Genesis 1:24-31

Materials: blue, green, flesh color, brown, yellow, and white felt; thin cardboard; glue; scissors; magnet strip

Instructions:

1. Photocopy patterns. Cut photocopied patterns out. Trace **1** on thin cardboard. Cut out.
2. Trace **2** on blue felt. Trace **3** on green felt. Trace **4** and **5** on flesh colored felt (or brown if desired). Trace **6** on brown felt. Trace **7** on yellow felt. Trace **8** on white felt. Cut out.
3. Cut out **9** and color.
4. Glue **2** on cardboard backing. Glue remaining pieces onto craft using finished illustration as guide.
5. Attach a strip of magnet to the back of the craft.

Creation Day 7

Scripture: Genesis 2:1-3

Materials: gold, blue, and green felt; thin cardboard; glue; scissors; magnet strip

Instructions:

1. Photocopy patterns. Cut photocopied patterns out. Trace **1** on thin cardboard.
2. Trace **2** on gold felt. Trace **3** on blue felt. Trace **4** on green felt. Cut out.
3. Cut out **5** and color.
4. Glue **2** on cardboard backing. Glue remaining pieces onto craft using finished illustration as guide.
5. Attach a strip of magnet to the back of the craft.

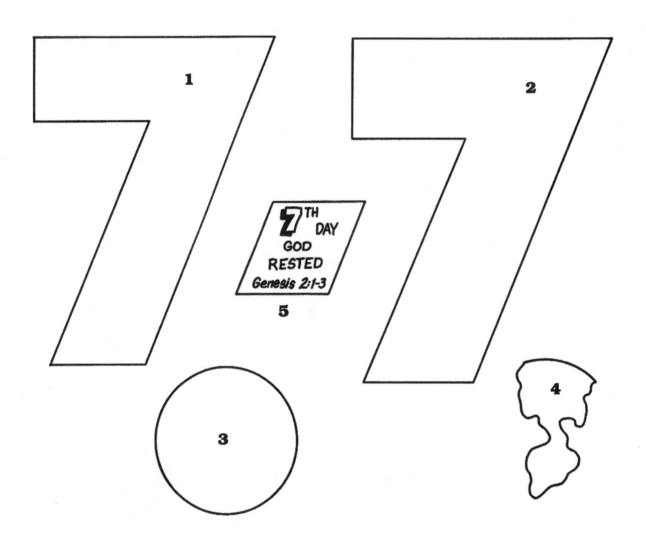

Scripture: Genesis 1

Materials: yellow, black, and various colored felt pieces; thin cardboard; glue; scissors; craft stamen; magnet strip

Instructions:

1. Photocopy patterns. Cut photocopied patterns out. Trace **1** on thin cardboard. Cut out.
2. Trace **2** on yellow felt. Trace **3** on black felt. Trace **4** on felt color of choice. Trace **5** and **6** on felt colors of choice. Flip **5** and **6** over and trace on same colors. Trace **7** and **8** twice on colors of choice. Cut out.
3. Cut out **9** and color same as **4**.
4. Glue **2** on cardboard backing. For butterfly antennae, fold craft stamen in half and glue onto back of **3**. Glue **3** on top of **2**. Glue remaining pieces onto craft using finished illustration as guide.
5. Attach a strip of magnet to the back of the craft.

Spring Flower

Scripture: Genesis 1

Materials: green, white, and yellow felt; thin cardboard; glue; scissors; magnet strip

Instructions:

1. Photocopy patterns. Cut photocopied patterns out. Trace **1** on thin cardboard. Cut out.
2. Trace **2** on green felt. Trace **3** on white felt. Trace **4** on yellow felt. Cut out.
3. Cut out **5** and color.
4. Glue **2** and **3** on cardboard backing. Allow white petal to overlap green leaf on the left side. Allow green leaf on the right side to overlap white petal. Glue remaining pieces onto craft using finished illustration as guide.
5. Attach a strip of magnet to the back of the craft.

Scripture: Genesis 1:16

Materials: dark blue and yellow felt; thin cardboard; glue; scissors; magnet strip

Instructions:

1. Photocopy patterns. Cut photocopied patterns out. Trace **1** on thin cardboard. Cut out.
2. Trace **2** on dark blue felt. Trace **3** on yellow felt. Cut out.
3. Cut out **4** and color.
4. Glue **2** on cardboard backing. Glue remaining pieces onto craft using finished illustration as guide.
5. Attach a strip of magnet to the back of the craft.

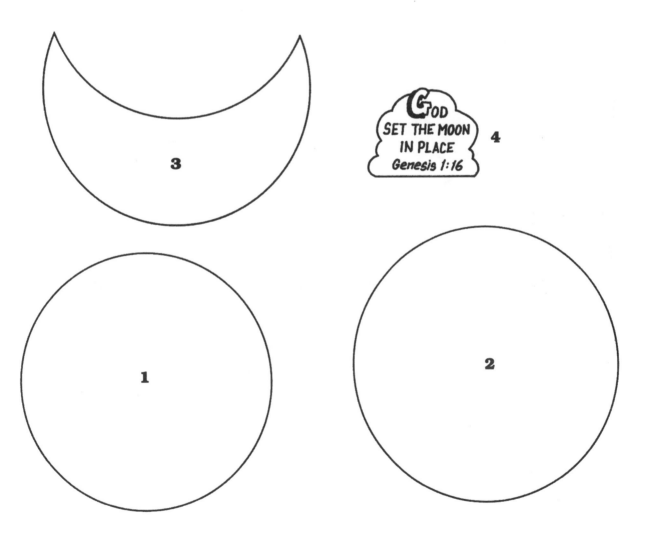

3

GOD SET THE MOON IN PLACE Genesis 1:16 **4**

1

2

Sea Horse

Scripture: Genesis 1:20

Materials: brown and gold felt; thin cardboard; glue; scissors; two craft eyes; magnet strip

Instructions:
1. Photocopy patterns. Cut photocopied patterns out. Trace **1** on thin cardboard and cut out.
2. Trace **2** once on brown felt and once on gold felt. Cut out.
3. Cut out **3** and color.
4. Glue one of the sea horses to **1**. Glue the other sea horse slightly offset on top of first seahorse. Glue craft eyes and label onto craft using finished illustration as guide.
5. Attach a strip of magnet to the back of the craft.

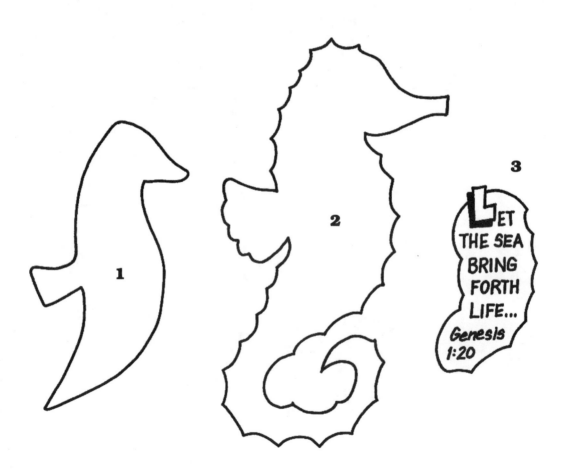

Scripture: Genesis 1:24

Materials: brown and green felt; thin cardboard; glue; scissors; for eye use either black felt and a hole punch or a craft eye; magnet strip

Instructions:

1. Photocopy patterns. Cut patterns out. Trace **1** on thin cardboard and cut out.

2. Trace **2** on brown felt. Trace **3-9** on green felt. Cut out.
3. Cut out **10** and color.
4. Use a hole punch on black felt for eye or use a craft eye.
5. Glue **2** on cardboard backing. Glue remaining pieces onto craft using finished illustration as guide.
6. Attach a strip of magnet to the back of the craft.

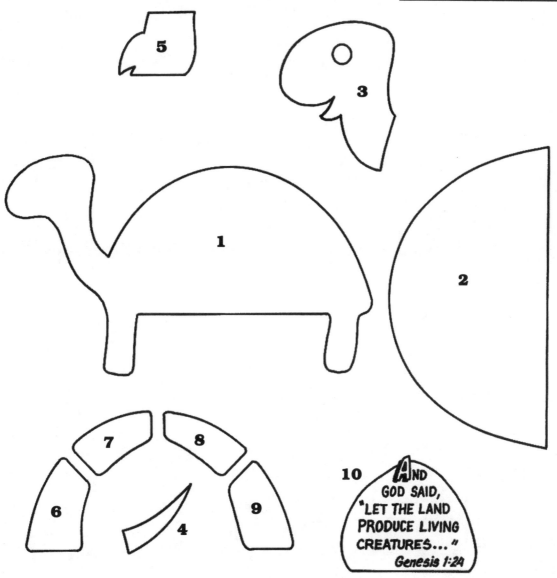

Dog

Scripture: Genesis 1:25

Materials: brown, red, and black felt; thin cardboard; glue; scissors; for eyes use black felt and a hole punch or craft eyes; magnet strip

Instructions:

1. Photocopy patterns. Cut patterns out. Trace **1** on thin cardboard and cut out.
2. Trace **2** on brown felt. Trace **3** on red felt. Trace **4** on black felt. Cut out.
3. Cut out **5** and color.
4. Use a hole punch on black felt for eye or use a craft eye.
5. Glue **2** on cardboard backing. Glue remaining pieces onto craft using finished illustration as guide.
6. Attach a strip of magnet to the back of the craft.

Scripture: Genesis 11:1-9

Materials: orange and brown felt; thin cardboard; glue; scissors; magnet strip

Instructions:

1. Photocopy patterns. Cut photocopied patterns out. Trace **1** on thin cardboard. Cut out.

2. Trace **2** on brown felt. Trace **3-7** on orange felt. Cut out.

3. Cut out **8** and color.

4. Glue **2** on cardboard backing. Glue remaining pieces onto craft using finished illustration as guide.

5. Attach a strip of magnet to the back of the craft.

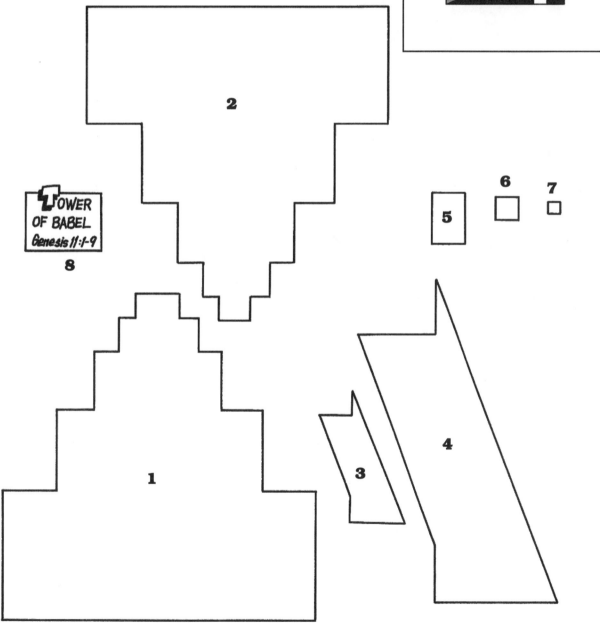

Hammer

Scripture: Genesis 6:5-12

Materials: brown, grey, flesh color, and blue felt; thin cardboard; glue; scissors; magnet strip

Instructions:
1. Photocopy patterns. Cut photocopied patterns out. Trace **1** on thin cardboard. Cut out.
2. Trace **2** on brown felt. Trace **3** on blue felt. Trace **4** on grey felt. Trace **5** on flesh color (or brown) felt. Cut out.
3. Cut out **6** and color.
4. Glue **2** on cardboard backing. Glue remaining pieces onto craft using finished illustration as guide.
5. Attach a strip of magnet to the back of the craft.

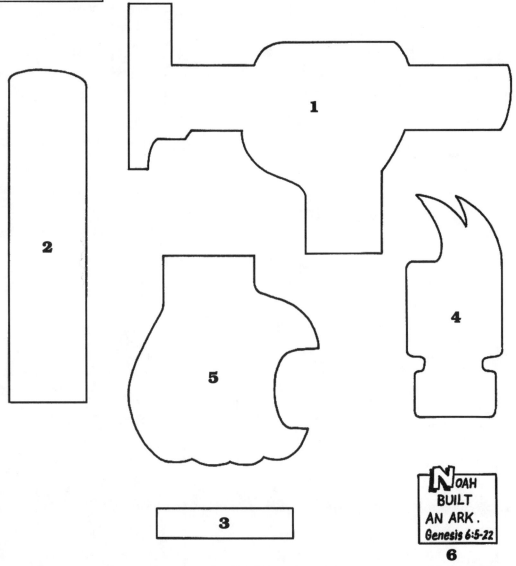

Noah's Ark

Scripture: Genesis 6:14

Materials: brown, red, light brown, yellow, blue, and black felt; thin cardboard; glue; scissors; magnet strip

Instructions:

1. Photocopy patterns. Cut photocopied patterns out. Trace **1** on thin cardboard. Cut out.
2. Trace **2** on brown felt. Trace **3**, **5**, and **10** on red felt. Trace **4** and **6** on light brown felt. Trace **7** on black felt. Trace **8** on yellow felt. Trace **9** on blue felt. Cut out.
3. Cut out **11** on color.
4. Glue **2** on cardboard backing. Glue remaining pieces onto craft using finished illustration as guide.
5. Attach a strip of magnet to the back of the craft.

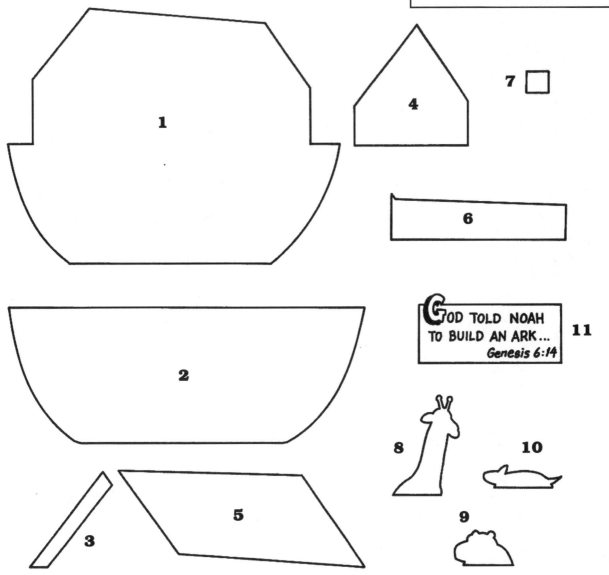

Umbrella

Scripture: Genesis 7:11-12

Materials: red, white, black, and blue felt; thin cardboard; glue; scissors; magnet strip

Instructions:

1. Photocopy patterns. Cut photocopied patterns out. Trace **1** on thin cardboard and cut out.
2. Trace **2** and **4** on red felt. Trace **3** and **5** on white felt. Trace **6** and **7** on black felt. Trace **8** and **9** on blue felt. Cut out.
3. Cut out **10-12** and color.
4. Glue **2-5** on cardboard backing. Glue remaining pieces onto craft using finished illustration as guide.
5. Attach a strip of magnet to the back of the craft.

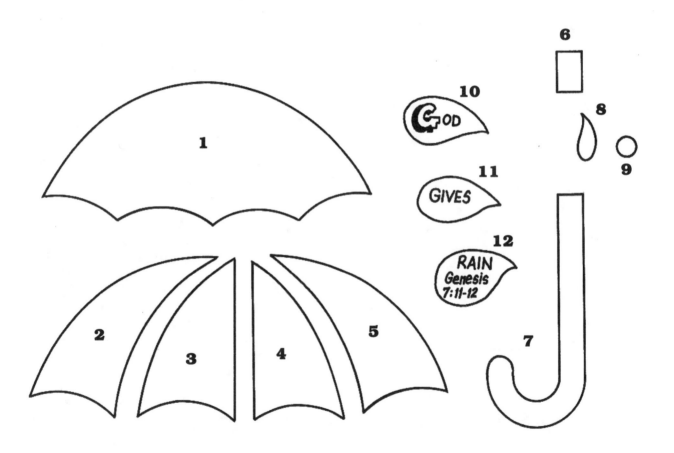

Dove

Scripture: Genesis 8:8

Materials: white, green, and brown felt; thin cardboard; glue; scissors; magnet strip

Instructions:

1. Photocopy patterns. Cut photocopied patterns out. trace **1** on thin cardboard and cut out.
2. Trace **2** and **3** on white felt. Trace **4-6** on green felt. Trace **7** on brown. Cut out.
3. Cut out **8** and color.
4. Glue **2** on cardboard backing. Glue remaining pieces onto craft using finished illustration as guide.
5. Attach a strip of magnet to the back of the craft.

8

NOAH SENT OUT A DOVE. Genesis 8:8

3

1

7

2

4

5

6

Rainbow

Scripture: Genesis 9:13

Materials: pink, blue, green, yellow and purple fabric; thin cardboard; glue; scissors; magnet strip

Instructions:

1. Photocopy patterns. Cut photocopied patterns out. Trace **1** on thin cardboard and cut out.

2. Trace **2** on pink felt. Trace **3** on blue felt. Trace **4** on green felt. Trace **5** on yellow felt. Trace **6** on purple felt. Cut out.

3. Cut out **7** and color.

4. Glue **2** on cardboard backing. Glue remaining pieces onto craft using finished illustration as guide.

5. Attach a strip of magnet to the back of the craft.

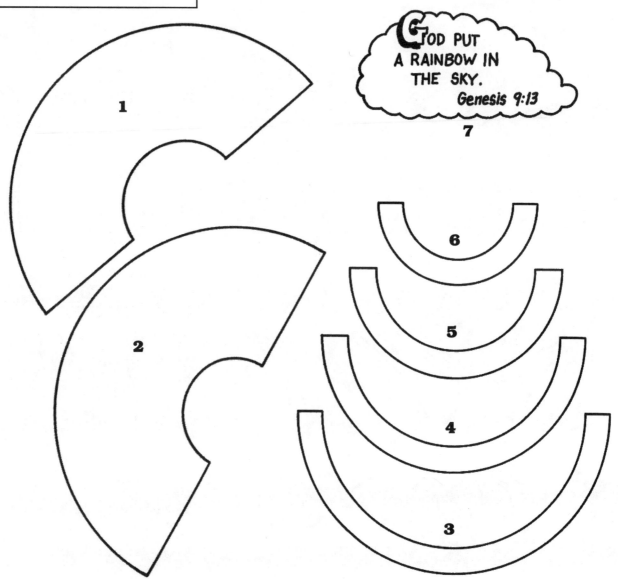

Joseph's Coat

Scripture: Genesis 37:3, 4

Materials: yellow felt; variety of colors for stripes in coat; thin cardboard; glue; scissors; magnet strip

Instructions:

1. Photocopy patterns. Cut patterns out. Trace **1** on thin cardboard and cut out.

2. Trace **2, 7, 20** and **21** on yellow felt. Trace **3-6, 8-16,** and **17-19** on felt color of choice. Cut out.

3. Cut out **22** and color.

4. Glue **2** on cardboard backing. Glue remaining pieces onto craft using finished illustration as guide.

5. Attach a strip of magnet to the back of the craft.

JOSEPH'S COAT OF MANY COLORS.

Joseph's Coat

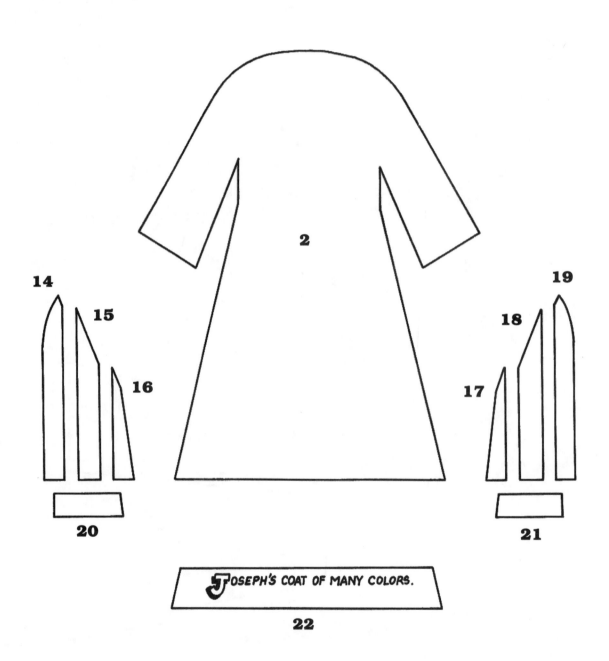

14

15

16

2

17

18

19

20

21

22

JOSEPH'S COAT OF MANY COLORS.

The Burning Bush

Scripture: Exodus 3:1-10

Materials: brown, green, and orange felt; thin cardboard; glue; scissors; magnet strip

Instructions:

1. Photocopy patterns. Cut photocopied patterns out. Trace **1** on thin cardboard and cut out.

2. Trace **2** on brown felt. Trace **3** on green felt. Trace **4** on orange felt. Cut out.
3. Cut out **5** and color.
4. Glue **4** on cardboard backing. Glue **3** on top of **4**. Glue remaining pieces onto craft using finished illustration as guide.
5. Attach a strip of magnet to the back of the craft.

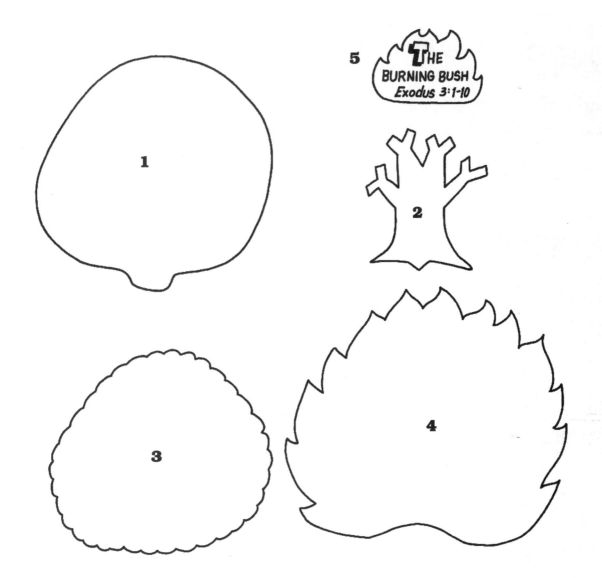

The Ten Commandments

Scripture: Exodus 20:1-17

Materials: black and gray felt; thin cardboard; glue; scissors; magnet strip

Instructions:

1. Photocopy patterns. Cut photocopied patterns out. Trace **1** on thin cardboard and cut out.
2. Trace **2** on black felt. Trace **3** twice on gray felt. Cut out.
3. Cut out **4** and color.
4. Glue **2** onto cardboard backing. Glue remaining pieces onto craft using finished illustration as guide.
5. Attach a strip of magnet to the back of the craft.

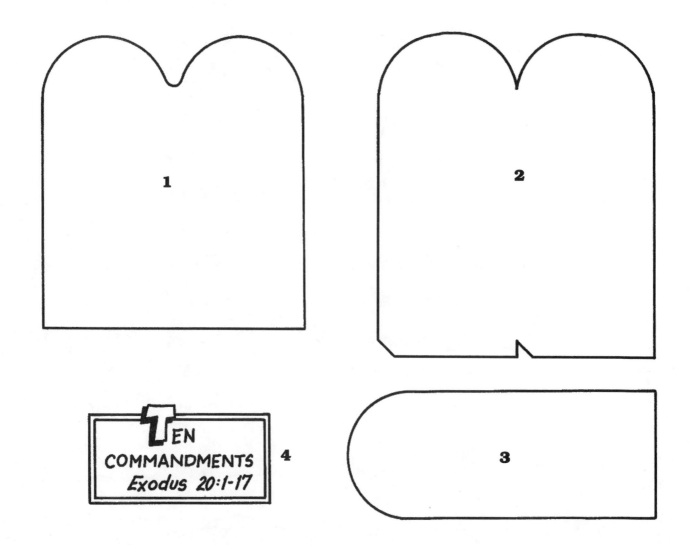

Scripture: Joshua 24:15

Materials: red, brown, and white felt; thin cardboard; glue; scissors; magnet strip

Instructions:

1. Photocopy patterns. Cut photocopied patterns out. Trace **1** on thin cardboard and cut out.
2. Trace **2** and **6** on red felt.

Trace **3** and **8** on brown felt. Trace **4** and **5** on white felt. Trace **7** twice on felt color of choice. Cut out.

3. Cut out **9** and color.
4. Glue **2** on cardboard backing. Glue remaining pieces onto craft using finished illustration as guide.
5. Attach a strip of magnet to the back of the craft.

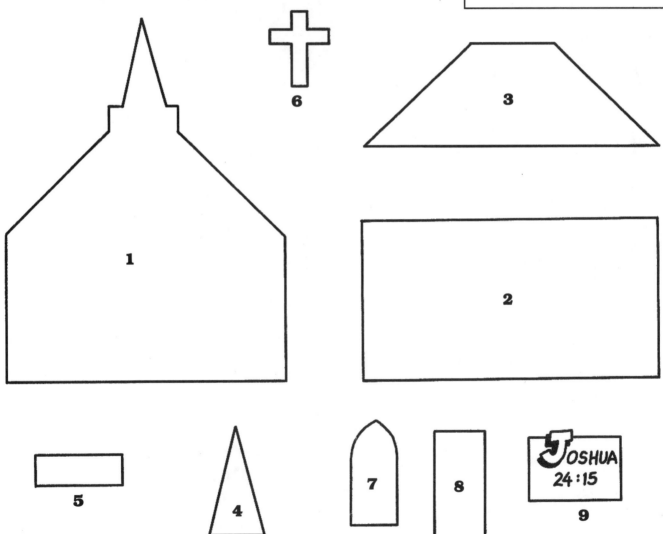

Harp

Scripture: Psalm 33:3

Materials: brown and white felt; thin cardboard; glue; string; scissors; magnet strip

Instructions:

1. Photocopy patterns. Cut photocopied patterns out. Trace **1** on thin cardboard and cut out.
2. Trace **2** on brown felt. Trace **3** on white felt. Cut out.
3. Cut out **4** and color.
4. Using dots on **3** as guide, glue nine 2 ¼" pieces of string on top of **3**.
5. Glue **2** on cardboard backing. Glue remaining pieces onto craft using finished illustration as guide.
6. Attach a strip of magnet to the back of the craft.

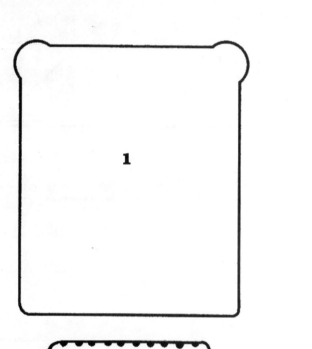

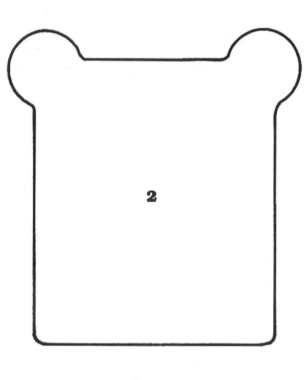

Mountain

Scripture: Psalm 66:5

Materials: light blue, orange, white, and purple felt; thin cardboard; glue; scissors; magnet strip

Instructions:

1. Photocopy patterns. Cut photocopied patterns out. trace **1** on thin cardboard and cut out.

2. Trace **2** and **3** on light blue felt. Trace **4** on orange felt. Trace **5** on white felt. Trace **6** on purple felt. Cut out.
3. Cut out **7** and color.
4. Glue **2** on cardboard backing. Glue remaining pieces onto craft using finished illustration as guide.
5. Attach a strip of magnet to the back of the craft.

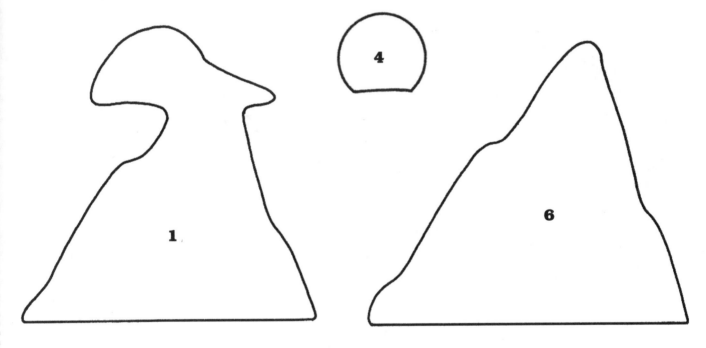

Sun

Scripture: Psalm 74:16

Materials: yellow and orange felt; thin cardboard; glue; scissors; magnet strip

Instructions:

1. Photocopy patterns. Cut photocopied patterns out. Trace **1** on thin cardboard and cut out.
2. Trace **1** again on orange felt. Trace **2** on yellow felt. Cut out.
3. Cut out **3** and color.
4. Glue **2** on cardboard backing. Glue remaining pieces onto craft using finished illustration as guide.
5. Attach a strip of magnet to the back of the craft.

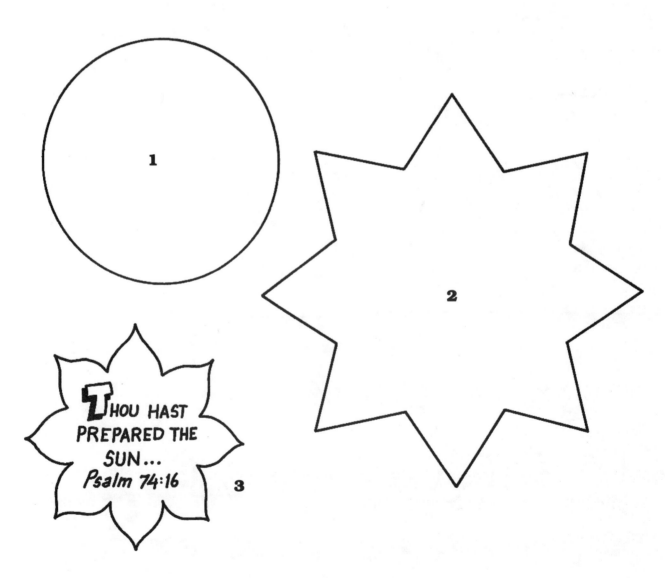

Scripture: Psalm 74:17

Materials: red and black felt; thin cardboard; glue; scissors; magnet strip

Instructions:

1. Photocopy patterns. Cut patterns out. Trace **1** on thin cardboard and cut out.
2. Trace **2-5** on red felt. Trace **6** on black felt. Trace **7** twice on black felt. Cut out.
3. Cut out **8** and color.
4. Glue **2** on cardboard backing. Glue remaining pieces onto craft using finished illustration as guide.
5. Attach a strip of magnet to the back of the craft.

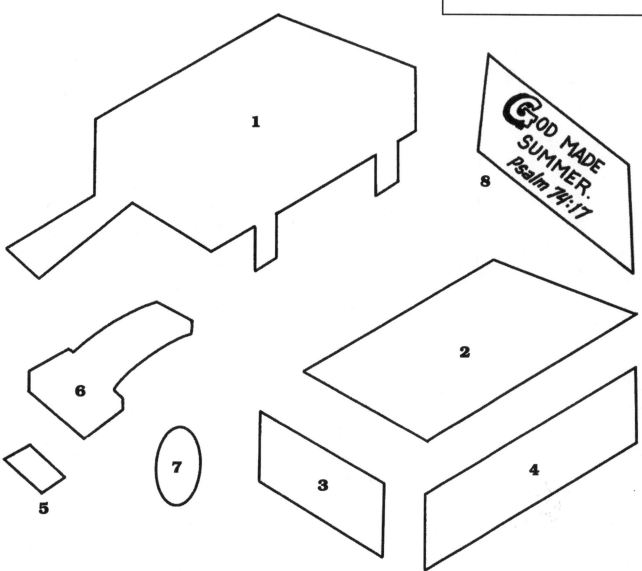

Pineapple

Scripture: Psalm 92:1

Materials: light brown, dark brown, and green felt; thin cardboard; glue; scissors; magnet strip

Instructions:

1. Photocopy patterns. Cut patterns out. Trace **1** on thin cardboard and cut out.
2. Trace **2** on light brown felt. Trace **3** on green felt. Trace **4** five times on dark brown felt. Cut out.
3. Cut out **5** and color.
4. Glue **2** on cardboard backing. Glue remaining pieces onto craft using finished illustration as guide.
5. Attach a strip of magnet to the back of the craft.

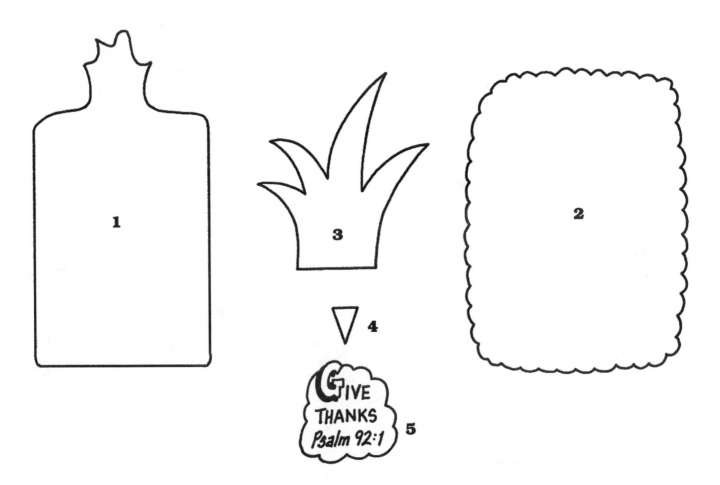

Scripture: Psalm 100:1

Materials: white, black, and red felt; thin cardboard; glue; scissors; magnet strip

Instructions:
1. Photocopy patterns. Cut patterns out. Trace **1** on thin cardboard and cut out.
2. Trace **2** on white felt.

Trace **3** twice on black felt. Trace **4** five times on black felt. **5** and **6** on red felt. Cut out.
3. Cut out **7** and color.
4. Glue **2** on cardboard backing. Glue remaining pieces onto craft using finished illustration as guide.
5. Attach a strip of magnet to the back of the craft.

5

6

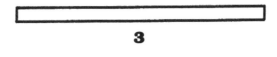

3

7

1

2

4

Scripture: Psalm 119:105

Materials: white and orange felt; thin cardboard; glue; scissors; magnet strip

Instructions:

1. Photocopy patterns. Cut patterns out. Trace **1** on thin cardboard and cut out.

2. Trace **2** on white felt. Trace **3** on orange felt. Cut out.
3. Cut out **5** and color.
4. Glue **2** on cardboard backing. Glue remaining pieces onto craft using finished illustration as guide.
5. Attach a strip of magnet to the back of the craft.

5

1

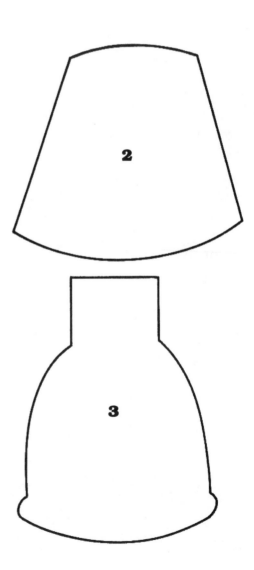

2

3

4

Tennis Shoe

Scripture: Psalm 119:133

Materials: white, red, blue, gold (or yellow), and black felt; thin cardboard; glue; scissors; magnet strip

Instructions:

1. Photocopy patterns. Cut patterns out. Trace **1** on thin cardboard and cut out.
2. Trace **2** on white felt. Trace **3**, **8**, and **10** on red felt. Trace **4**, **5**, **6**, **9**, and **11** on blue felt. Trace **7** on gold or yellow felt. Trace **8** on black felt.. Trace **7** and **8** six times. Cut out patterns.
3. Cut out **12** and color.
4. Glue **2** on cardboard backing. Glue remaining pieces onto craft using finished illustration as guide.
5. Attach a strip of magnet to the back of the craft.

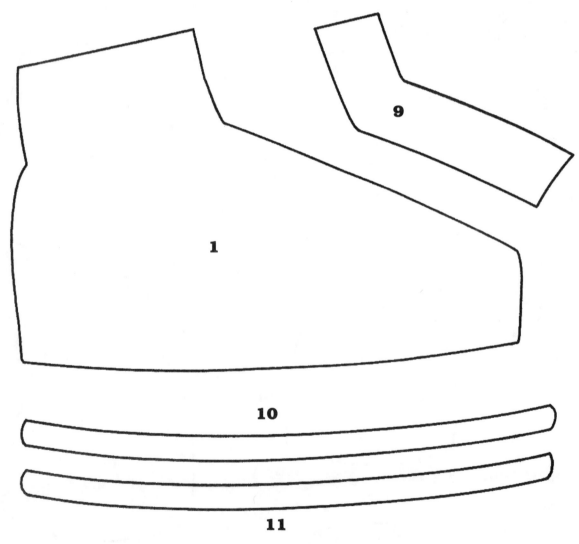

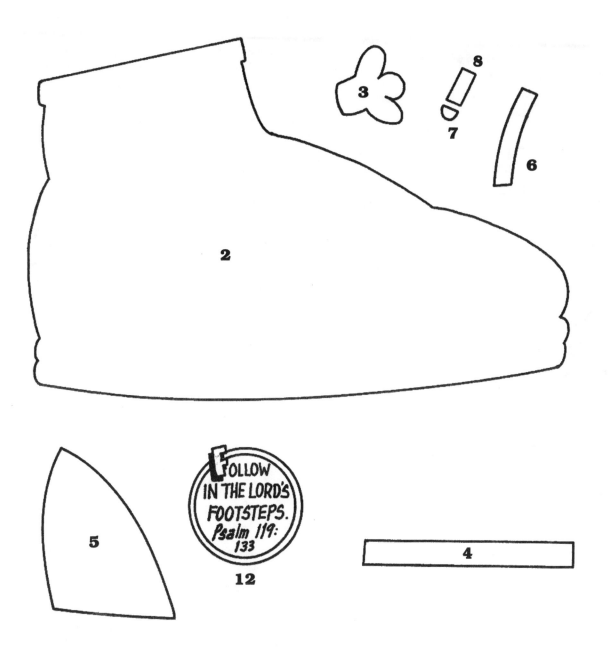

FOLLOW IN THE LORD'S FOOTSTEPS. Psalm 119: 133

Jonah and the Great Fish

Scripture: Jonah 1-3

Materials: blue, light blue, and white felt; thin cardboard; glue; scissors; magnet strip

Instructions:

1. Photocopy patterns. Cut patterns out. Trace **1** on thin cardboard and cut out.
2. Trace **2** on light blue felt. Trace **3** and **6** on white felt. Trace **4** and **5** on blue felt. Cut out.
3. Cut out **7** and color.
4. Glue **2** on cardboard backing. Glue remaining pieces onto craft using finished illustration as guide.
5. Attach a strip of magnet to the back of the craft.

Saw

Scripture: Matthew 1:18-25

Materials: grey and red felt; thin cardboard; glue; scissors; magnet strip

Instructions:

1. Photocopy patterns. Cut patterns out. Trace **1** on thin cardboard and cut out.
2. Trace **2** on red felt. Trace **3** on grey felt. Cut out.
3. Cut out **4** and color.
4. Glue **2** on cardboard backing. Glue remaining pieces onto craft using finished illustration as guide.
5. Attach a strip of magnet to the back of the craft.

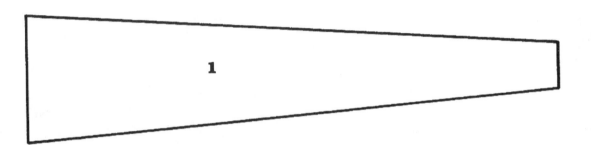

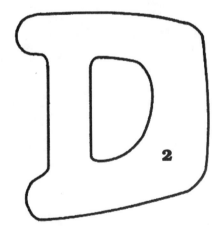

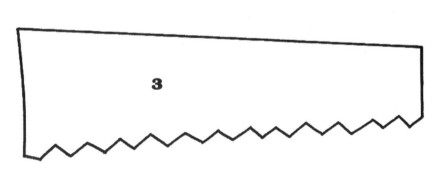

Fish

Scripture: Matthew 4:19

Materials: blue, gold, and pink felt; thin cardboard; glue; scissors; for eye use either black felt and a hole punch or a craft eye; magnet strip

Instructions:

1. Photocopy patterns. Cut patterns out. Trace **1** on thin cardboard and cut out.
2. Trace **2** and **7** on pink felt.

Trace **7** six times. Trace **3**, **4**, and **5** on gold felt. Trace **6** on blue felt. Cut out.
3. Cut out **9** and color.
4. Use a hole punch on black felt for **8** or use a craft eye.
5. Glue **5** and **6** on cardboard backing. Glue remaining pieces onto craft using finished illustration as guide.
6. Attach a strip of magnet to the back of the craft.

Scripture: Matthew 6:9-13

Materials: black and orange felt; thin cardboard; glue; scissors; magnet strip

Instructions:

1. Photocopy patterns. Cut patterns out. Trace **1** on thin cardboard and cut out.

2. Trace **2**, **3** and **6** on black felt. Trace **4** and **5** on orange felt. Cut out.
3. Cut out **7** and color.
4. Glue **2** on cardboard backing. Glue remaining pieces onto craft using finished illustration as guide.
5. Attach a strip of magnet to the back of the craft.

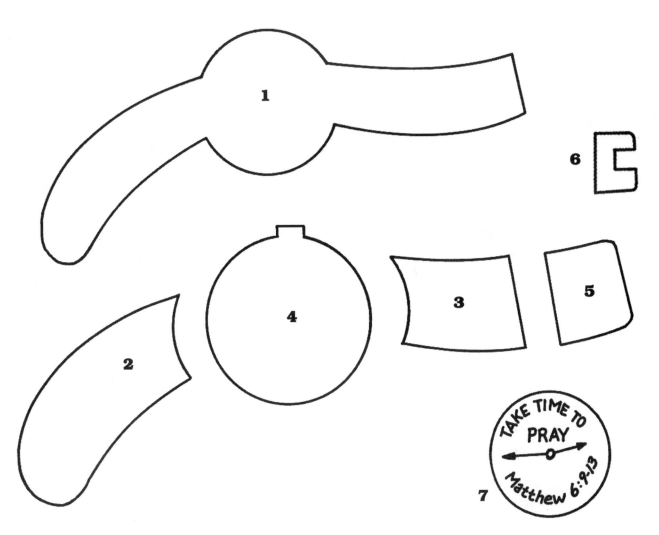

Shirt

Scripture: Matthew 6:25-34

Materials: red and yellow felt; thin cardboard; glue; scissors; magnet strip

Instructions:

1. Photocopy patterns. Cut patterns out. Trace **1** on thin cardboard and cut out.
2. Trace **2-5** and **9** on red felt. Trace **6-8** on yellow felt. Trace **7** five times. Cut out.
3. Cut out **10** and color.
4. Glue **2** and **3** on cardboard backing. Glue remaining pieces onto craft using finished illustration as guide.
5. Attach a strip of magnet to the back of the craft.

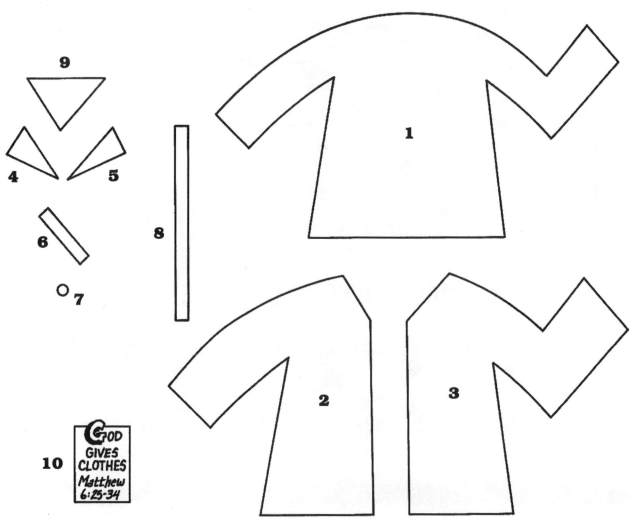

Ice Cream Cone

Scripture: Matthew 6:24, 25

Materials: tan, white, pink, and red felt; thin cardboard; glue; scissors; hole punch; magnet strip

Instructions:

1. Photocopy patterns. Cut patterns out. Trace **1** on thin cardboard and cut out.
2. Trace **2** on tan felt. Trace **3** on white felt. Trace **4** on pink felt. Cut out. Use a hole punch on red felt for the sprinkles on the ice cream.
3. Cut out **5** and color.
4. Glue **2** on cardboard backing. Glue remaining pieces onto craft using finished illustration as guide.
5. Attach a strip of magnet to the back of the craft.

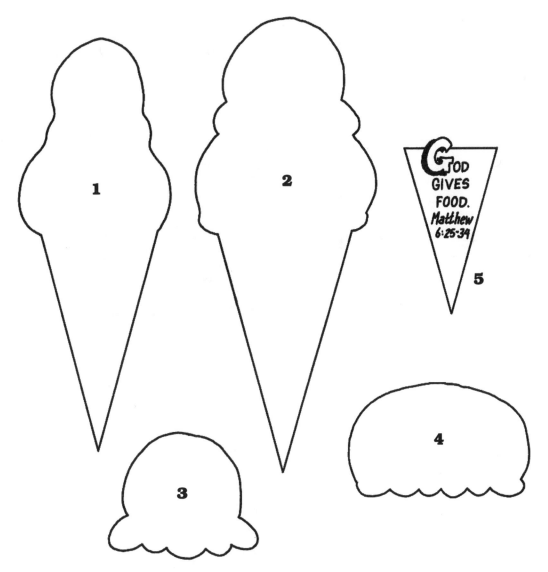

Jesus Calms the Seas

Scripture: Matthew 8:23-27

Materials: blue, dark blue, yellow, purple, and dark purple felt; thin cardboard; glue; scissors; magnet strip

Instructions:
1. Photocopy patterns. Cut patterns out. Trace **1** on thin cardboard and cut out.
2. Trace **2** on blue felt. Trace **3** on dark blue felt. Trace **4** on yellow felt. Trace **5** on dark purple felt. Trace **6** on purple felt. Cut out.
3. Cut out **7** and color.
4. Glue **2** and **5** on cardboard backing. Glue **4** on top of **2** and **5**. Glue remaining pieces onto craft using finished illustration as guide
5. Attach a strip of magnet to the back of the craft.

Key

Scripture: Matthew 16:19

Materials: yellow and gold felt; thin cardboard; glue; scissors; magnet strip

Instructions:

1. Photocopy patterns. Cut patterns out. Trace **1** on thin cardboard and cut out.

2. Trace **2** on gold felt. Trace **3-5** on orange felt. Cut out.

3. Cut out **6** and color.

4. Glue **2** on cardboard backing. Glue remaining pieces onto craft using finished illustration as guide.

5. Attach a strip of magnet to the back of the craft.

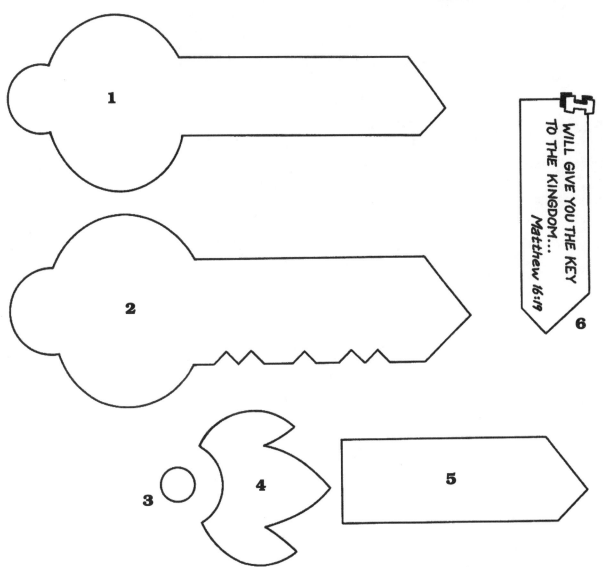

Traffic Light

Scripture: Luke 8:26-29; John 4:7-27

Materials: black, red, yellow, and green felt; thin cardboard; glue; scissors; magnet strip

Instructions:

1. Photocopy patterns. Cut patterns out. Trace **1** on thin cardboard and cut out.
2. Trace **2** on black felt. Trace **3** once on red felt, once on yellow felt, and once on green felt. Cut out.
3. Cut out **4** and color red. Cut out **5** and color yellow. Cut out **6** and color green.
4. Glue **2** on cardboard backing. Glue remaining pieces onto craft using finished illustration as guide.
5. Attach a strip of magnet to the back of the craft.

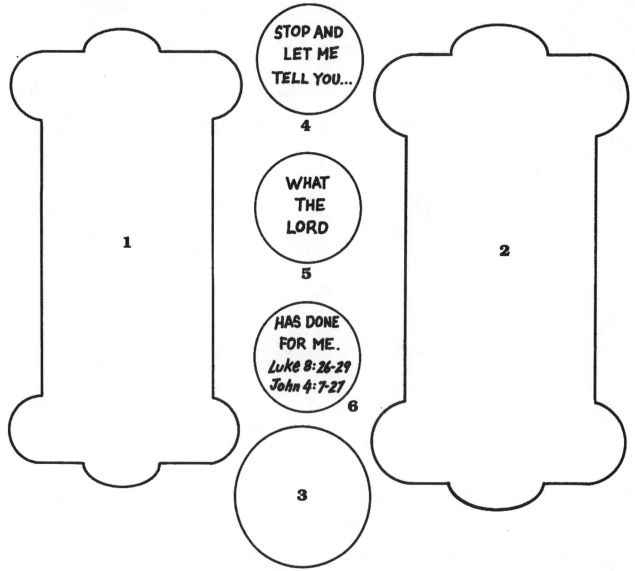

Scripture: Luke 10:2

Materials: yellow, brown, red and orange felt; thin cardboard; glue; scissors; magnet strip

Instructions:

1. Photocopy patterns. Cut patterns out. Trace **1** on thin cardboard and cut out.

2. Trace **2** and **5** on yellow felt. Trace **3** on brown felt. Trace **4** on orange felt. Trace **6** on red felt. Cut out.

3. Cut out **7** and color.

4. Glue **2** on cardboard backing. Glue remaining pieces onto craft using finished illustration as guide.

5. Attach a strip of magnet to the back of the craft.

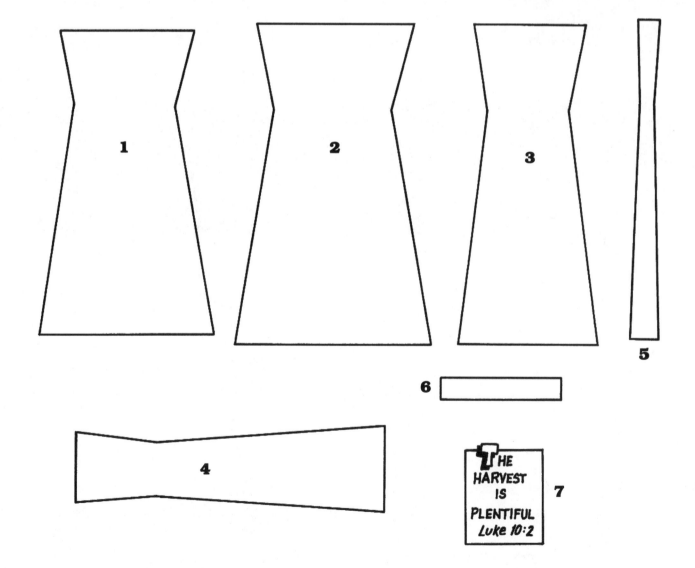

Zaccheus Tree

Scripture: Luke 19:1-10

Materials: brown, green, and dark green felt; thin cardboard; glue; scissors; magnet strip

Instructions:

1. Photocopy patterns. Cut patterns out. Trace **1** on thin cardboard and cut out.
2. Trace **2** and **5** on brown felt. Trace **3** on green felt. Trace **4** on dark green felt. Cut out.
3. Cut out **6** and color.
4. Glue **4** on cardboard backing. Glue remaining pieces onto craft using finished illustration as guide.
5. Attach a strip of magnet to the back of the craft.

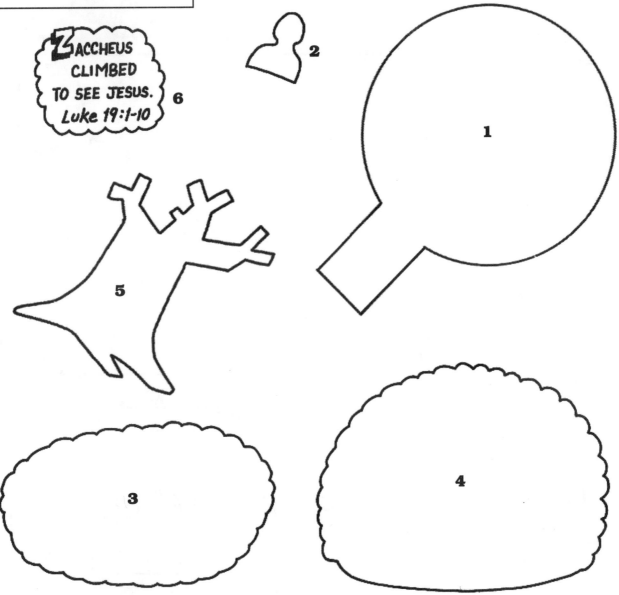

Scripture: John 4:10

Materials: red, orange, green and yellow felt; thin cardboard; glue; scissors; magnet strip

Instructions:

1. Photocopy patterns. Cut patterns out. Trace **1** on thin cardboard and cut out.

2. Trace **2** on yellow felt. Trace **3-5** on red felt. Trace **6** on green felt. Trace **7** eight times on red. Cut out.

3. Cut out **8** and color.

4. Glue **2** on cardboard backing. Glue remaining pieces onto craft using finished illustration as guide.

5. Attach a strip of magnet to the back of the craft.

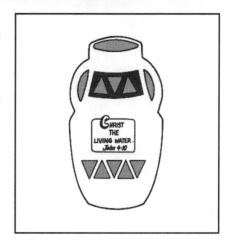

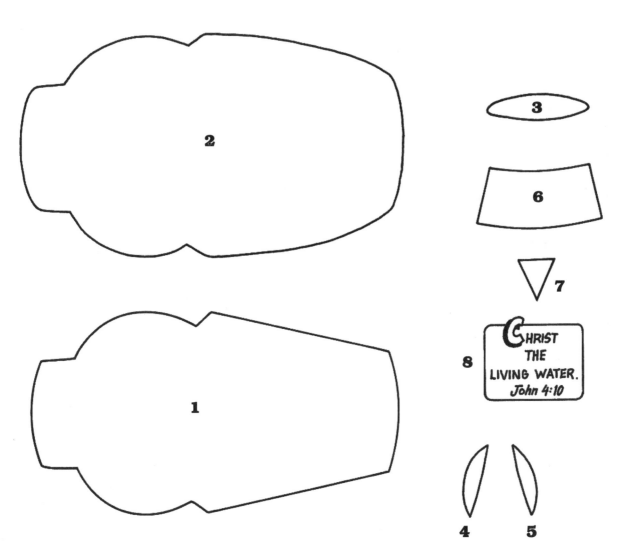

Mailbox

Scripture: John 3:16

Materials: red, grey, black, and brown felt; thin cardboard; glue; scissors; magnet strip

Instructions:

1. Photocopy patterns. Cut patterns out. Trace **1** on thin cardboard and cut out.
2. Trace **2** on grey felt. Trace **3** on red felt. Trace **4** and **6** on black felt. Trace **5** on brown felt. Cut out.
3. Cut out **7** and color.
4. Glue **5** on cardboard backing. Glue remaining pieces onto craft using finished illustration as guide.
5. Attach a strip of magnet to the back of the craft.

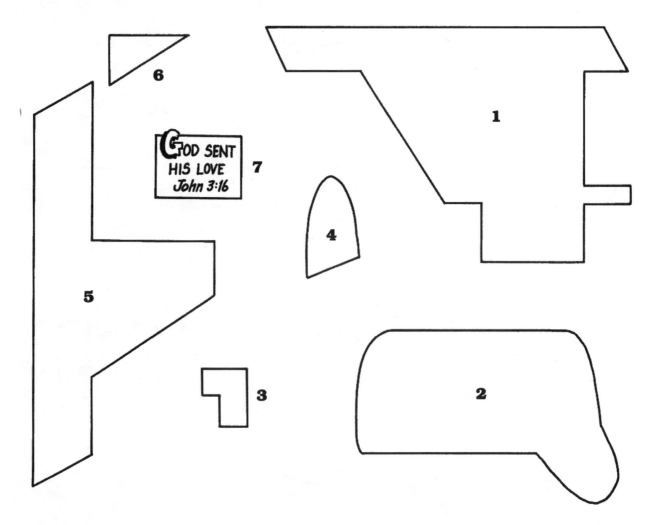

Kite

Scripture: Luke 8:26-29

Materials: brown and red felt; thin cardboard; glue; scissors; string; magnet strip

Instructions:

1. Photocopy patterns. Cut patterns out. Trace **1** on thin cardboard and cut out.
2. Trace **2** on brown felt. Trace **3-7** on red felt. Cut out.
3. Cut out **8** and color.
4. Attach a 5" string to bottom point of craft. Glue **7** to string
4. Glue **2** on cardboard backing. Glue remaining pieces onto craft using finished illustration as guide.
5. Attach a strip of magnet to the back of the craft.

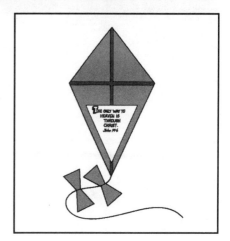

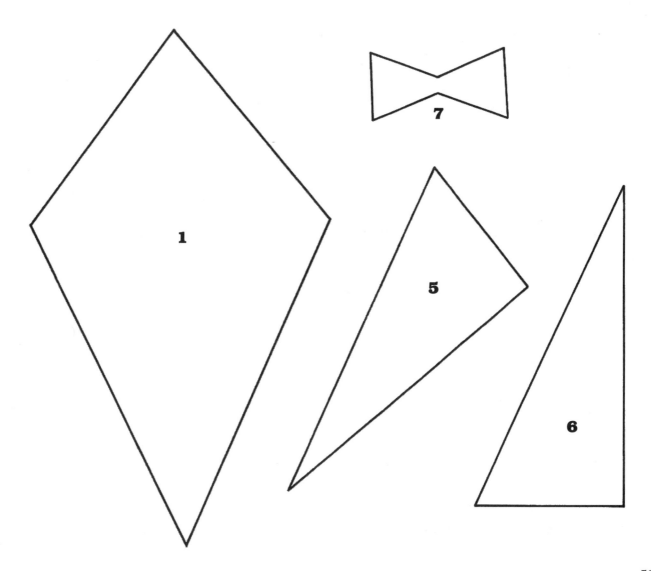

1

7

5

6

Kite

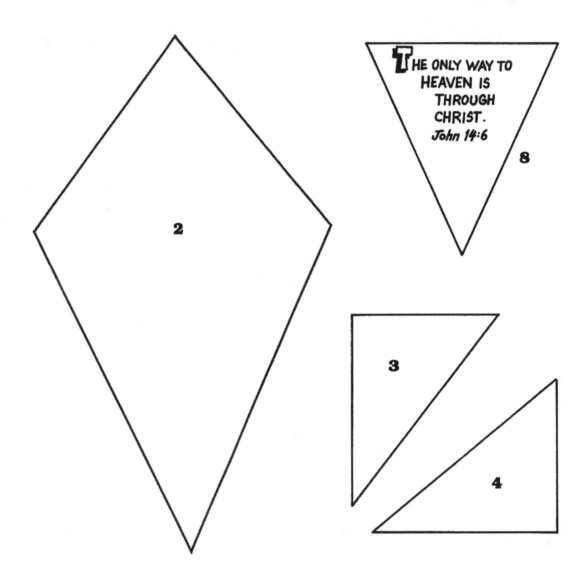

The only way to heaven is through Christ. John 14:6

2

8

3

4

Stained Glass Window

Scripture: Acts 2:42

Materials: black, blue, yellow, pink and green felt; thin cardboard; glue; scissors; magnet strip

Instructions:
1. Photocopy patterns. Cut patterns out. Trace **1** on thin cardboard and cut out.
2. Trace **2** on black felt.

Trace **3-5** on yellow felt. Trace **6** and **11** on blue felt. Trace **7** and **8** on pink felt. Trace **9** and **10** on green felt. Cut out.
3. Cut out **12** and color.
4. Glue **2** on cardboard backing. Glue remaining pieces onto craft using finished illustration as guide.
5. Attach a strip of magnet to the back of the craft.

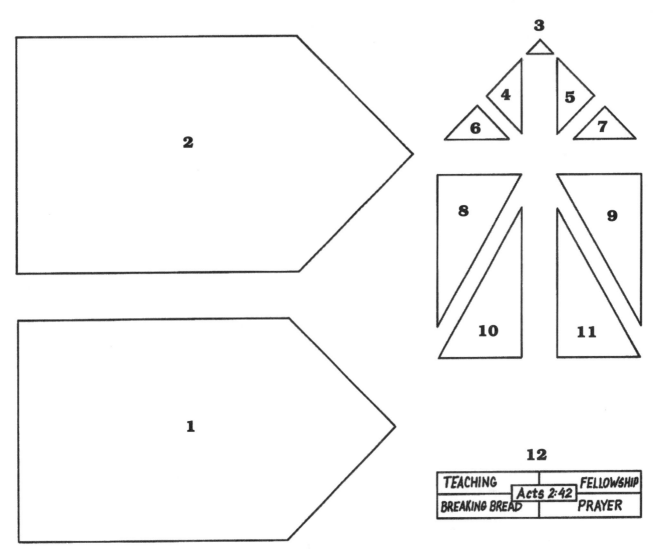

Crown

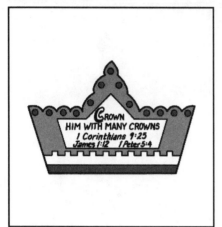

Scripture: 1 Corinthians 9:25; James 1:12; 1 Peter 5:4

Materials: gold, blue, and orange felt; thin cardboard; glue; scissors; hole punch; magnet strip

Instructions:

1. Photocopy patterns. Cut patterns out. Trace **1** on thin cardboard and cut out.
2. Trace **2** on gold felt. Trace **3** on blue felt. Trace **4** on orange felt. Cut out.
3. Cut out **5** and color.
4. Using a hole punch, punch out pieces from the orange and blue felt for jewels along the top of the crown.
5. Glue **2** on cardboard backing. Glue remaining pieces onto craft using finished illustration as guide.
6. Attach a strip of magnet to the back of the craft.

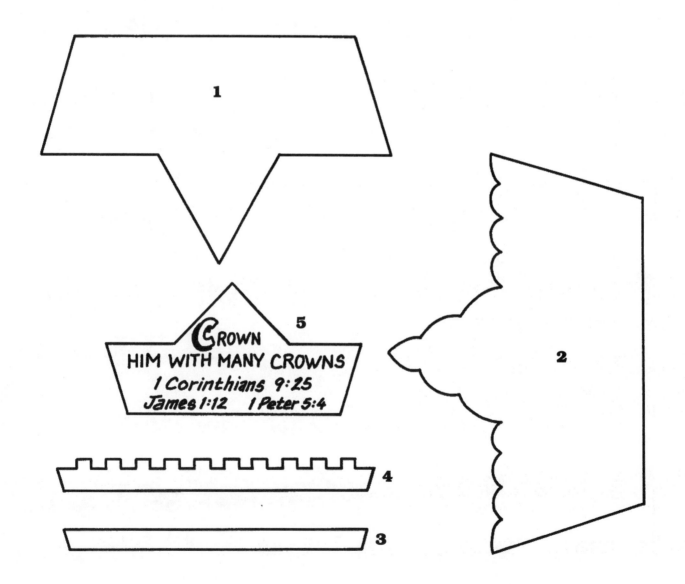

Teapot

Scripture: 1 Corinthians 10:31

Materials: yellow, pink, and orange felt; thin cardboard; glue; scissors; magnet strip

Instructions:

1. Photocopy patterns. Cut patterns out. Trace **1** on thin cardboard and cut out.

2. Trace **2** on orange felt. Trace **3-6** on yellow felt. Trace **7** and **8** on pink felt. Cut out.

3. Cut out **9** and color.

4. Glue **2** on cardboard backing. Glue remaining pieces onto craft using finished illustration as guide.

5. Attach a strip of magnet to the back of the craft.

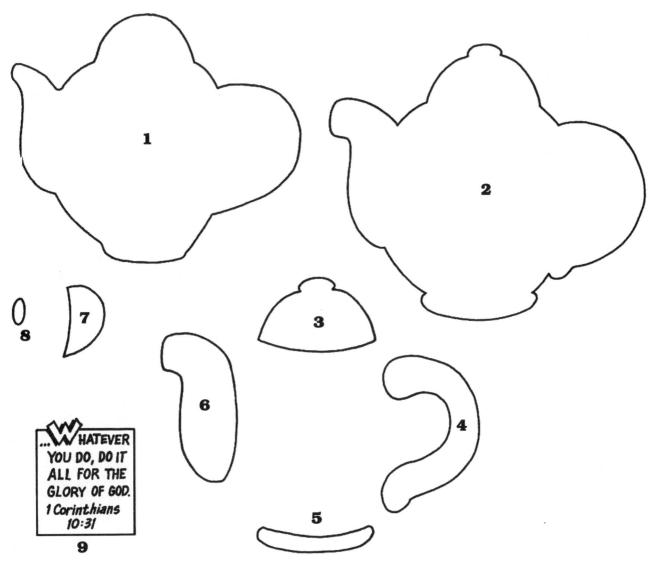

Fruit of the Spirit

Scripture: Galatians 5:22-23

Materials: red, brown, and green felt; thin cardboard; glue; scissors; magnet strip

Instructions:

1. Photocopy patterns. Cut patterns out. Trace **1** on thin cardboard and cut out.
2. Trace **2** on red felt. Trace **3** on brown felt. Trace **4** on green felt. Cut out.
3. Cut out **5** and color.
4. Glue **2** on cardboard backing. Glue remaining pieces onto craft using finished illustration as guide.
5. Attach a strip of magnet to the back of the craft.

Bee

Scripture: Ephesians 4:33

Materials: black, yellow and light blue felt; thin cardboard; glue; scissors; for eye use either black felt and a hole punch or a craft eye; magnet strip

Instructions:

1. Photocopy patterns. Cut patterns out. Trace **1** on thin cardboard and cut out.
2. Trace **2** on yellow felt.

Trace **3-6** on black felt. Trace **7** and **8** on light blue felt. Cut out.

3. Cut out **9** and color.
4. Use a hole punch on black felt for eyes or use a craft eyes.
5. Glue **8** on cardboard backing. Glue **2** on top of **8**. Glue remaining pieces onto craft using finished illustration as guide.
6. Attach a strip of magnet to the back of the craft.

Leaf

Scripture: Colossians 1:15

Materials: brown and orange felt; thin cardboard; glue; scissors; magnet strip

Instructions:
1. Photocopy patterns. Cut patterns out. Trace **1** on thin cardboard and cut out.
2. Trace **2** on brown felt.

Trace **3** on orange felt.
Note: You might want to use a variety of other warm colors like red or yellow. Cut out.
3. Cut out **4** and color.
4. Glue **2** on cardboard backing. Glue remaining pieces onto craft using finished illustration as guide.
5. Attach a strip of magnet to the back of the craft.

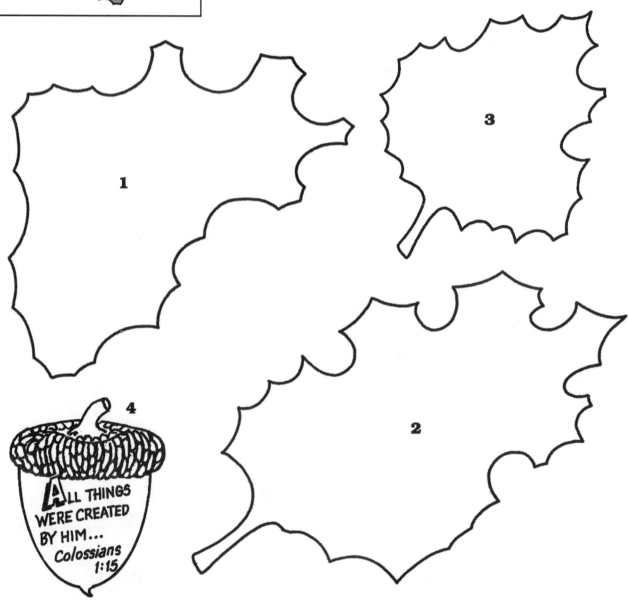

Scripture: 2 Timothy 2:15

Materials: pink, gold, orange, and black felt; thin cardboard; glue; scissors; hole punch; magnet strip

Instructions:
1. Photocopy patterns. Cut patterns out. Trace **1** on thin cardboard and cut out.
2. Trace **2** on pink felt. Trace **3** and **5** on gold felt. Trace **4** on orange felt. Trace **6** on black felt. Cut out. Use a hole punch on pink felt for **7**.
3. Cut out **8** and color.
4. Glue **2** on cardboard backing. Glue remaining pieces onto craft using finished illustration as guide.
5. Attach a strip of magnet to the back of the craft.

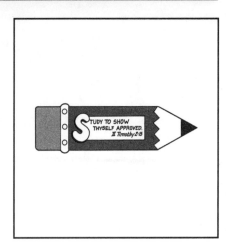

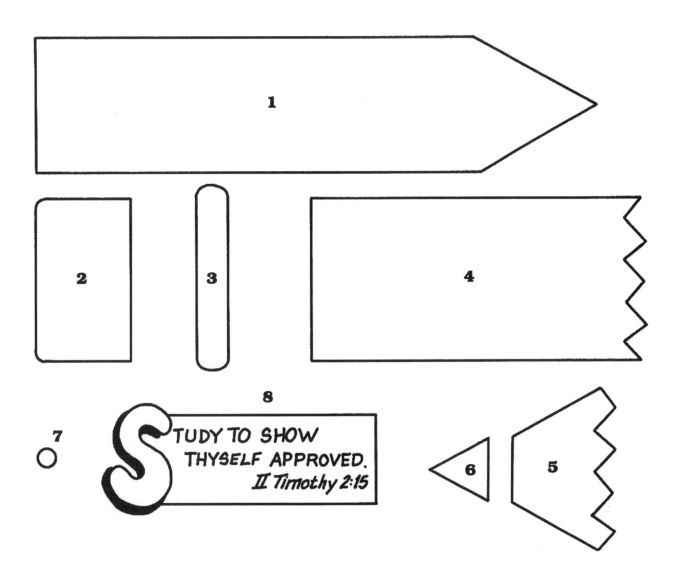

Bear

Scripture: 1 Peter 2:24

Materials: brown, red, tan, and black felt; thin cardboard; glue; scissors; for eyes use either black felt and a hole punch or craft eyes; magnet strip

Inatructions:

1. Photocopy patterns. Cut patterns out. Trace **1** on thin cardboard and cut out.

2. Trace **2** on brown felt. Trace **3**, **4**, **6**, and **7** on tan felt. Trace **5** on black felt. Trace **8** and **9** on red felt. Cut out.
3. Cut out **10** and color.
4. Use a hole punch on black felt for eye or use a craft eye.
5. Glue **2** on cardboard backing. Glue remaining pieces onto craft using finished illustration as guide.
6. Attach a strip of magnet to the back of the craft.

Scripture: 1 John 4:10

Materials: black, white, and yellow felt; thin cardboard; glue; scissors; magnet strip

Instructions:

1. Photocopy patterns. Cut patterns out. Trace **1** on thin cardboard and cut out.
2. Trace **1** again, except this time on black felt. Trace **2** and **3** on white felt. Trace **4** twice on yellow felt. Cut out.
3. Cut out **5** and **6**. Do not color.
4. Glue **2** on cardboard backing. Glue remaining pieces onto craft using finished illustration as guide.
5. Attach a strip of magnet to the back of the craft.

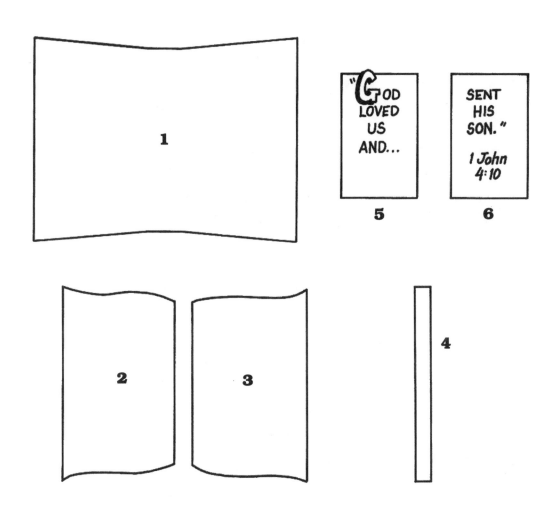

Picture Frame

Scripture: 1 John 4:16

Materials: yellow, brown, and red felt; thin cardboard; glue; scissors; magnet strip

Instructions:

1. Photocopy patterns. Cut patterns out. Trace **1** on thin cardboard and cut out.
2. Trace **2** on yellow felt. Trace **3** and **4** twice on brown felt. Trace **5** on red felt. Cut out.
3. Cut out **6** and color.
4. Glue **2** on cardboard backing. Glue remaining pieces onto craft using finished illustration as guide.
5. Attach a strip of magnet to the back of the craft.

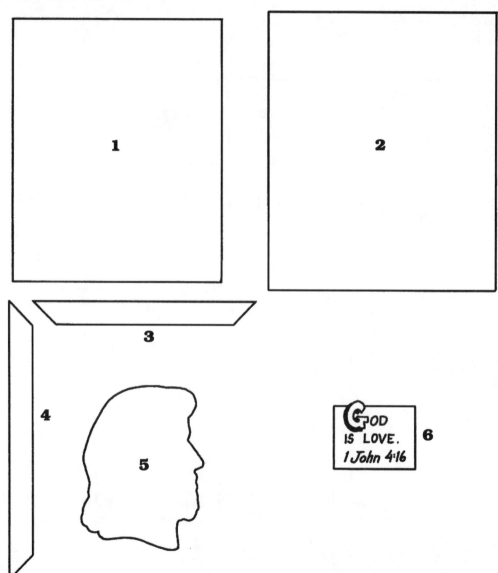

Scripture: Revelation 4:11

Materials: yellow and orange felt; thin cardboard; glue; scissors; magnet strip

Instructions:
1. Photocopy patterns. Cut patterns out. Trace **1** on thin cardboard and cut out.
2. Trace **1** again, except this time on orange felt. Trace **2** four times on yellow felt. Cut out.
3. Cut out **3** and color.
4. Glue **1** on cardboard backing. Glue a petal on every other outside flap. Glue remaining piece on center of craft.
5. Attach a strip of magnet to the back of the craft.

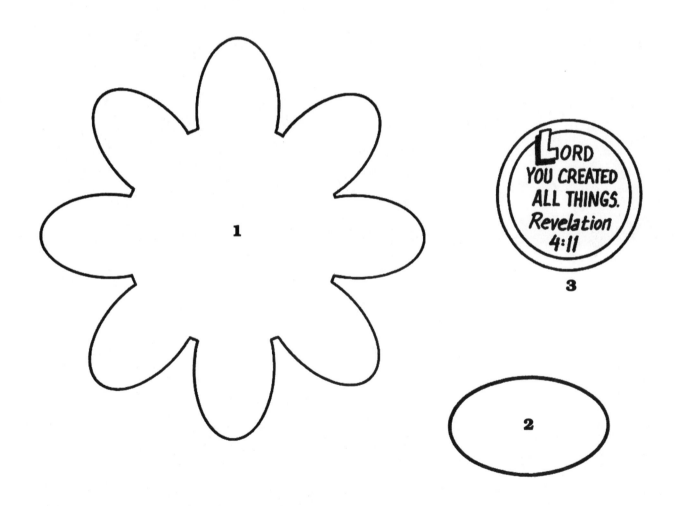

Tulip

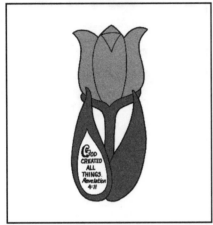

Scripture: Revelation 4:11

Materials: white, pink, dark pink, and green felt; thin cardboard; glue; scissors; magnet strip

Instructions:

1. Photocopy patterns. Cut patterns out. Trace **1** on thin cardboard and cut out.
2. Trace **2** on white felt. Trace **3** on pink felt. Trace **4** on dark pink felt. Trace **5-7** on green felt. Cut out.
3. Cut out **8** and color.
4. Glue **2** on cardboard backing. Glue remaining pieces onto craft using finished illustration as guide. When gluing on **4**, bend the top of the petal slightly outward to give it a three-dimensional effect.
5. Attach a strip of magnet to the back of the craft.

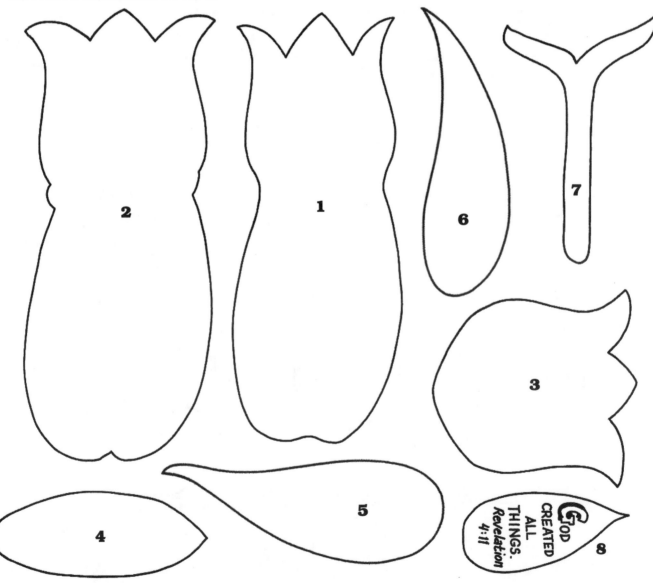

Valentine

Materials: red felt; glue; scissors

Instructions:
1. Photocopy pattern. Cut patterns out. Trace **1** four times on red felt and cut out.
2. Color **2-5** and cut out.
3. Glue a label to the center of each of the red hearts.
4. Give them to others as Valentines.

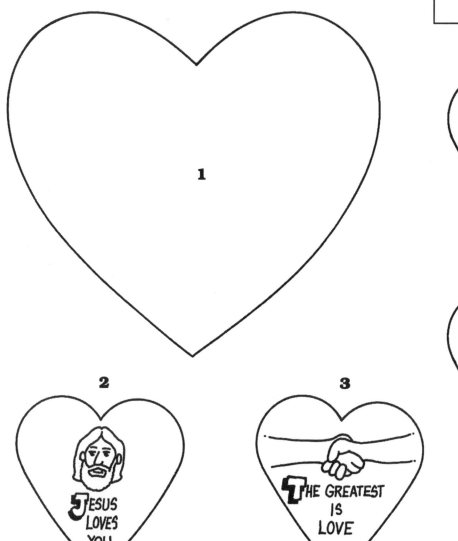

Happy Heart

Materials: red and white felt; thin cardboard; glue; scissors; aluminum foil; magnet strip

Instructions:

1. Photocopy patterns. Cut patterns out. Trace **1** on thin cardboard and cut out.
2. Trace **1** again except this time on white felt. Trace **2** on aluminum foil. Trace **3** on red felt. Cut out.
3. Cut out **4** and color.
4. Glue **1** on cardboard backing. Glue remaining pieces onto craft using finished illustration as guide.
5. Attach a strip of magnet to the back of the craft.

Mother's Day Violet

Materials: purple, yellow, green, and light green felt; thin cardboard; glue; scissors; chenille wire; magnet strip

Instructions:

1. Photocopy pattern. Cut patterns out. Trace **1** on thin cardboard and cut out.
2. Trace **2-6** on purple felt. Trace **7** on yellow felt. Trace **8** on green felt.. Trace **9** on light green felt.

3. Color **10** and cut out.
4. Glue chenille wire from center of thin cardboard pattern to the bottom where the leaves meet the plant.
5. Glue **2-6** on craft. Glue remaining pieces onto craft using finished illustration as guide.
6. Attach a strip of magnet to the back of the craft.

Cut out.

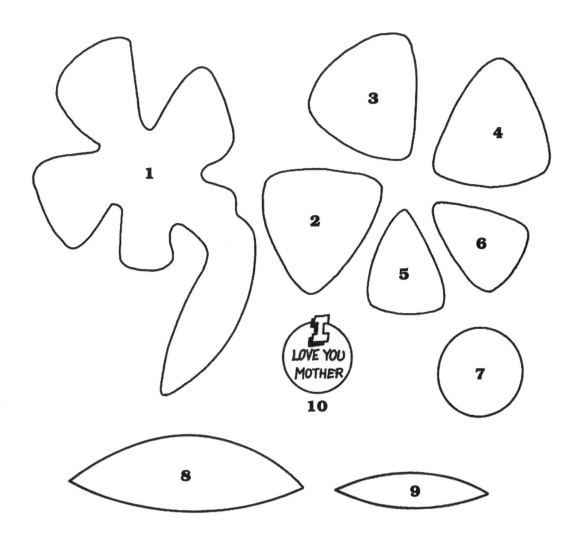

Father's Day Tie

Materials: light green, and yellow felt; thin cardboard; glue; scissors; magnet strip

Instructions:

1. Photocopy patterns. Cut patterns out. Trace **1** on thin cardboard and cut out.
2. Trace **2** on light green felt. Trace **3-7** on yellow felt. Cut out.
3. Cut out **8** and color.
4. Glue **2** on cardboard backing. Glue remaining pieces onto craft using finished illustration as guide.
5. Attach a strip of magnet to the back of the craft.

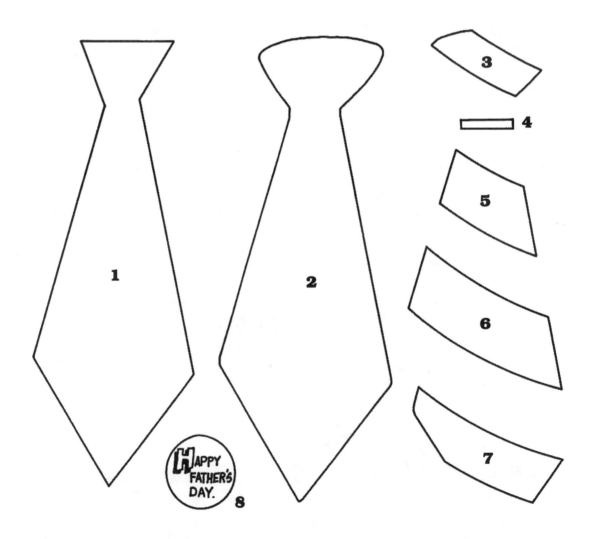

Materials: red, yellow, and blue felt; thin cardboard; glue; scissors; magnet strip

Instructions:

1. Photocopy patterns. Cut patterns out. Trace **1** on thin cardboard and cut out.
2. Trace **1** again, but this time on yellow felt. Trace **2** on red felt. Trace **3** on blue felt. Cut out.
3. Cut out **4** and color.
4. Glue **2** on cardboard backing. Glue remaining pieces onto craft using finished illustration as guide.
5. Attach a strip of magnet to the back of the craft.

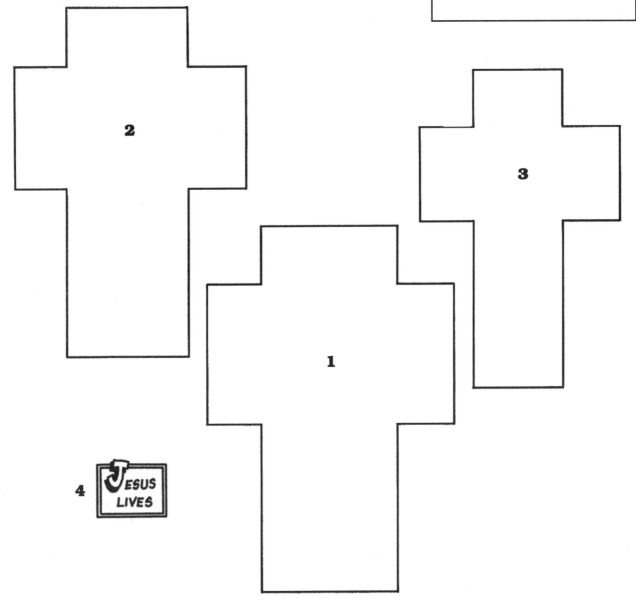

Cross

Materials: pink and light blue felt; thin cardboard; glue; scissors; magnet strip

Instructions:

1. Photocopy patterns. Cut patterns out. Trace **1** on thin cardboard and cut out.
2. Trace **1** again, except this time on pink felt. Trace **3** on pink felt also. Trace **2** on light blue felt. Cut out.
3. Cut out **4** and color.
4. Glue **1** on cardboard backing. Glue remaining pieces onto craft using finished illustration as guide.
5. Attach a strip of magnet to the back of the craft.

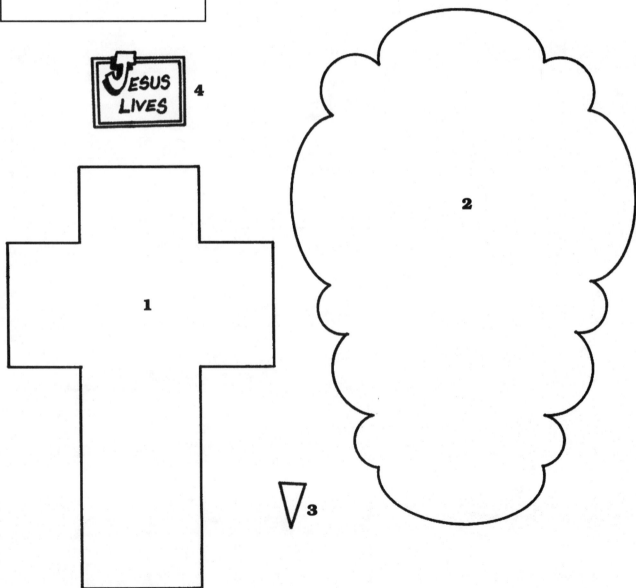

Easter Lily

Materials: white, green, and yellow felt; thin cardboard; glue; scissors; magnet strip

Instructions:

1. Photocopy patterns. Cut patterns out. Trace **1** on thin cardboard and cut out.
2. Trace **2-3** on white felt. Trace **4** on green felt. Trace **5-7** on yellow felt. Cut out.
3. Cut out **8** and color.
4. Glue **3** on cardboard backing. Glue remaining pieces onto craft using finished illustration as guide.
5. Attach a strip of magnet to the back of the craft.

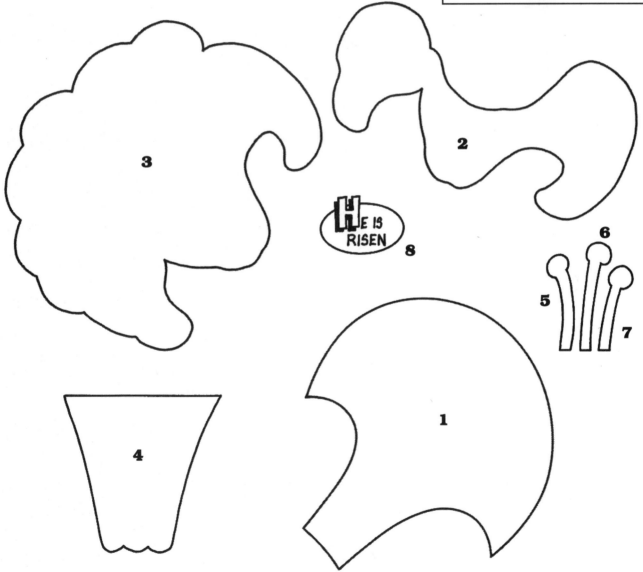

Horn of Plenty

Materials: brown, light brown, green, black, orange, yellow, red, and purple felt; thin cardboard; glue; scissors; magnet strip

Instructions:
1. Photocopy patterns. Cut patterns out. Trace **1** on thin cardboard and cut out.
2. Trace **2** on brown felt. Trace **3-5** on light brown felt. Trace **6** on green felt.

Trace **7** on black felt. Trace **8** on orange felt. Trace **9** and **12** on yellow felt. Trace **10** on red felt. Trace **11** on purple felt. Cut out.
3. Cut out **13** and color.
4. Glue **2** on cardboard backing. Glue remaining pieces onto craft using finished illustration as guide.
5. Attach a strip of magnet to the back of the craft.

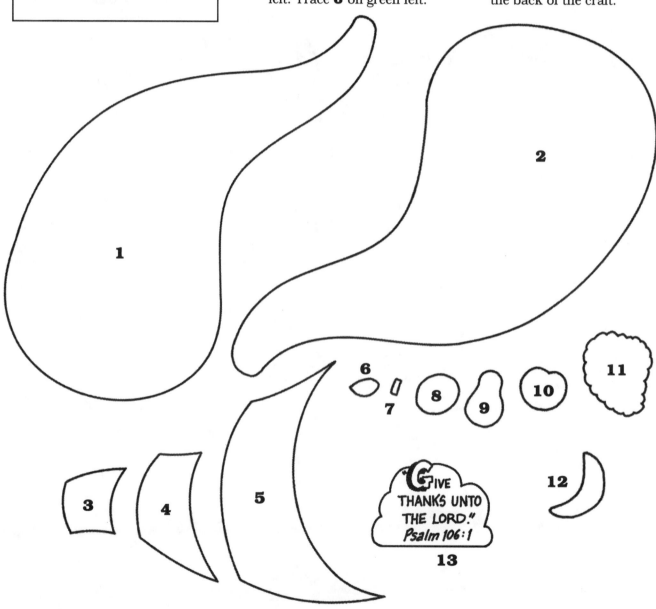

Baby Jesus in the Manger

Materials: brown, yellow, and white felt; thin cardboard; glue; scissors; magnet strip

Instructions:

1. Photocopy patterns. Cut patterns out. Trace **1** on thin cardboard and cut out.
2. Trace **2** on brown felt.

Trace **3** on yellow felt. Trace **4** on white felt. Cut out.
3. Cut out **5** and color.
4. Glue **2** on cardboard backing. Glue remaining pieces onto craft using finished illustration as guide.
5. Attach a strip of magnet to the back of the craft.

Candle

Materials: grey, red, green, white, yellow, and orange felt; thin cardboard; glue; scissors; magnet strip

Instructions:

1. Photocopy patterns. Cut patterns out. Trace **1** on thin cardboard and cut out.
2. Trace **1** again except this time on gray felt. Trace **2** and **4** on red felt. Trace **8** several times on red felt. Trace **5** on green felt. Trace **6** on yellow felt. Trace **7** on orange felt. Cut out.
3. Cut out **9** and color.
4. Glue grey felt **1** on cardboard backing. Glue remaining pieces onto craft using finished illustration as guide.
5. Attach a strip of magnet to the back of the craft.

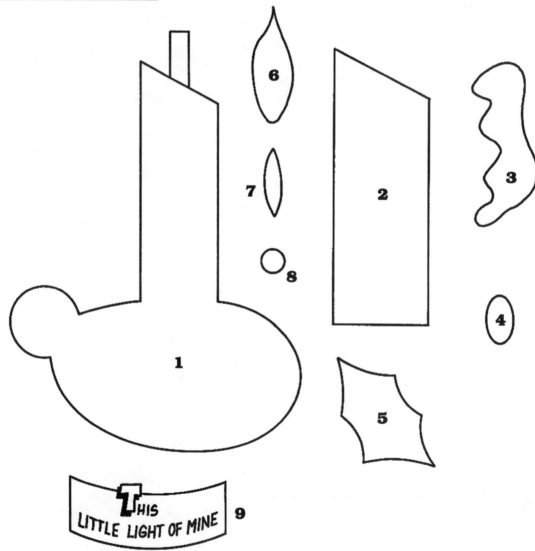

Christmas Tree

Materials: green, yellow, and red felt; thin cardboard; glue; scissors; hole punch; magnet strip

Instructions:

1. Photocopy patterns. Cut patterns out. Trace **1** on thin cardboard and cut out.
2. Trace **2** on green felt. Trace **3** on on red felt.

Trace **4-7** on yellow felt. Cut out. Using a hole punch, punch out several circles of various colors of felt to represent ornaments.

3. Cut out **8** and color.
4. Glue **2** on cardboard backing. Glue remaining pieces onto craft using finished illustration as guide.
5. Attach a strip of magnet to the back of the craft.

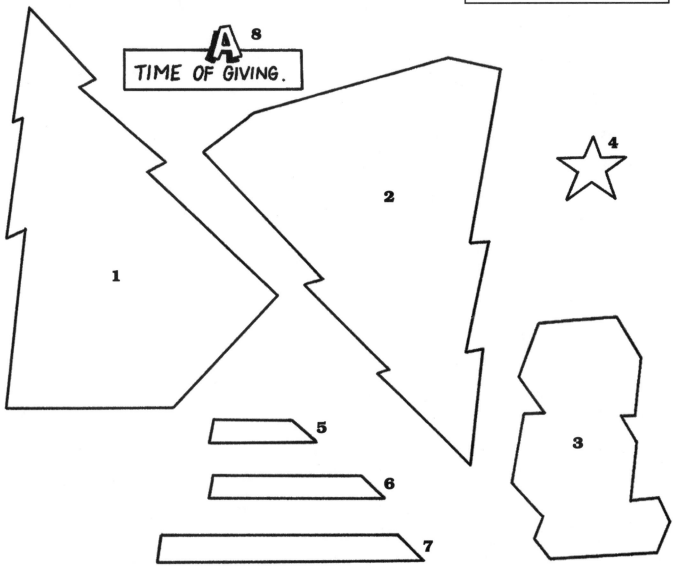

77

Bell

Materials: blue, yellow, and red felt; thin cardboard; glue; scissors; magnet strip

Instructions:

1. Photocopy patterns. Cut patterns out. Trace **1** on thin cardboard and cut out.

2. Trace **2** on blue felt. Trace **3** on yellow felt. Trace **4** on red felt. Cut out.

3. Glue **2** on cardboard backing. Glue remaining pieces onto craft using finished illustration as guide.

4. Attach a strip of magnet to the back of the craft.

Snowman

Materials: white, black, red, and orange felt; thin cardboard; glue; scissors; magnet strip

Instructions:

1. Photocopy patterns. Cut patterns out. Trace **1** on thin cardboard and cut out.
2. Trace **2** on white felt.

Trace **3** and **6-14** on black felt. Trace **4** on red felt. Trace **5** on orange felt. Cut out.

3. Glue **2** on cardboard backing. Glue remaining pieces onto craft using finished illustration as guide.
4. Attach a strip of magnet to the back of the craft.

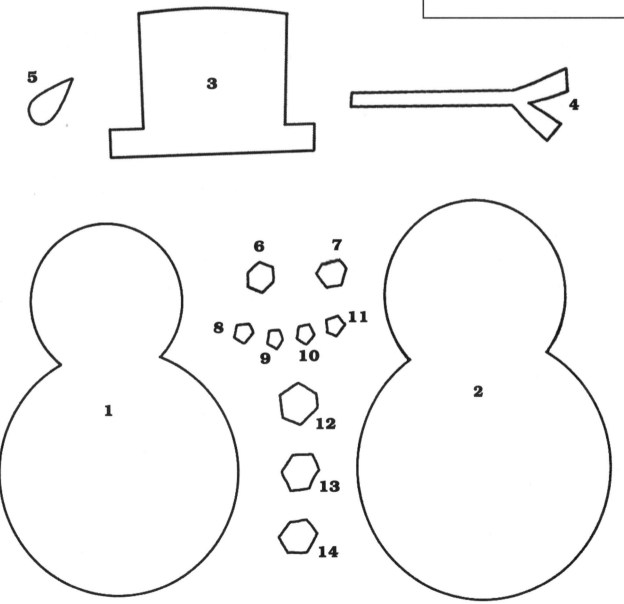

Scripture Index